This book belongs to

The twin prayers of this book are ancient prayers for morning and evening. They pray, praise, and give thanks to God for all his good gifts—his life, forgiveness, and salvation as well as his presence and care in our lives. These prayers use Psalm 31:5, Psalm 91:11, and Psalm 121. Our version of these ancient prayers is adapted from Martin Luther's *Small Catechism* (1529).

FatCat is hidden on every page. And so is Jesus! Jesus is present in his word, so look for where God's word is in each scene: perhaps there's a Bible somewhere or people are singing God's word. Wherever God's word is, there is Jesus with all his good gifts of life, forgiveness, and salvation!

Join the communion of saints in prayer, and let these words wash over your days and nights, commending yourself and all things to the Lord our God.

KEEP US THIS DAY

A Morning Prayer for All God's Children

Art by

Text by

Todd R. Hains

Our heavenly Father,

성경전서

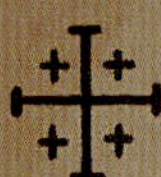

는 너를 애굽
종 되었던 집
서 인도하여 낸
의 하나님 여호
와로라
XODUS 20:2

we give you thanks through
your dear Son, Jesus Christ,

that you have kept us this night from all harm and danger.

We ask you to keep us this day also,
from all sin and evil,

나는 너를 애굽
땅 종 되었던 집
에서 인도하여
낸 너의 하나님
여호와로라
Exodus 20:2

that all our thoughts, words,
and deeds may please you.

Into your hands we commend ourselves, our bodies and souls, and all things.

Let your holy angels be with us,

버스 BUS

that the evil foe may have
no power over us.

온 땅이여 여호와께 기쁨으로 외쳐라
시편100

Amen.

I lift up my eyes to the hills. From where does my help come?
My help comes from the LORD, who made heaven and earth.
He will not let your foot be moved; he who keeps you will not slumber.
Behold, he who keeps Israel will neither slumber nor sleep.
The LORD is your keeper; the LORD is your shade on your right hand.
The sun shall not strike you by day, nor the moon by night.
The LORD will keep you from all evil; he will keep your life.
The LORD will keep your going out and your coming in from this time forth and forevermore.

Psalm 121

Amen.

that the evil foe may
have no power over us.

You LORD,
only, make me
dwell in safety.
Ps. 4:8

Let your holy angels
be with us,

Into your hands we commend
ourselves, our bodies and souls,
and all things.

HOLY

and to graciously
keep us this night.

We ask you to forgive us all our sins
and the wrongs that we have done

that you have graciously
kept us this day.

we give you thanks through
your dear Son, Jesus Christ,

Our heavenly Father,

KEEP US THIS NIGHT

An Evening Prayer for All God's Children

Art by
Natasha Kennedy

Text by
Todd R. Hains

יהוה שמה יהוה שמה יהוה שמה

The twin prayers of this book are ancient prayers for morning and evening. They pray, praise, and give thanks to God for all his good gifts—his life, forgiveness, and salvation as well as his presence and care in our lives. These prayers use Psalm 31:5, Psalm 91:11, and Psalm 121. Our version of these ancient prayers is adapted from Martin Luther's *Small Catechism* (1529).

FatCat is hidden on every page. And so is Jesus! Jesus is present in his word, so look for where God's word is in each scene: perhaps there's a Bible somewhere or people are singing God's word. Wherever God's word is, there is Jesus with all his good gifts of life, forgiveness, and salvation!

Join the communion of saints in prayer, and let these words wash over your days and nights, commending yourself and all things to the Lord our God.

Keep Us This Day, Keep Us This Night: A Morning Prayer and An Evening Prayer for All God's Children

Lexham Press, 1313 Commercial St., Bellingham, Washington 98225 | LexhamPress.com

ISBN 9781683598749 | Library of Congress Control Number 2024952412
24 25 26 27 28 29 30 / IN / 12 11 10 9 8 7 6 5 4 3 2 1

Also find Fat Cat
in these books!
THE KING OF EASTER
Jesus Searches for All God's Ch
THE KING OF CHRISTMAS
All God's Children Search for Jesus
THE APOSTLES' CREED
For All God's Children
THE LORD'S PRAYER
For All God's Children
THE TEN COMMANDMENTS
For All God's Children